The Super R

An American Pro

Scott Nearing

Alpha Editions

This edition published in 2024

ISBN : 9789364739115

Design and Setting By
Alpha Editions
www.alphaedis.com
Email - info@alphaedis.com

As per information held with us this book is in Public Domain.
This book is a reproduction of an important historical work. Alpha Editions uses the best technology to reproduce historical work in the same manner it was first published to preserve its original nature. Any marks or number seen are left intentionally to preserve its true form.

Contents

CHAPTER I THE CALL OF THE SUPER RACE .... - 1 -

CHAPTER II EUGENICS—THE SCIENCE OF RACE CULTURE .... - 6 -

CHAPTER III SOCIAL ADJUSTMENT—THE SCIENCE OF MOLDING INSTITUTIONS .... - 13 -

CHAPTER IV EDUCATION—THE SCIENCE OF INDIVIDUAL DEVELOPMENT .... - 18 -

CHAPTER V THE AMERICAN OPPORTUNITY .... - 26 -

Footnotes: ....- 32 -

CHAPTER I
THE CALL OF THE SUPER RACE

As a very small boy, I distinctly remember that stories of the discovery of America and Australia, of the exploration of Central Africa and of the invention of the locomotive, the steamboat, and the telegraph made a deep impression on my childish mind; and I shall never forget going one day to my mother and saying:—

"Oh, dear, I wish I had been born before everything was discovered and invented. Now, there is nothing left for me to do."

Brooding over it, and wondering why it should be so, my boyish soul felt deeply the tragedy of being born into an uneventful age. I fully believed that the great achievements of the world were in the past. Imagine then my joy when, in the course of my later studies, it slowly dawned upon me that the age in which I lived was, after all, an age of unparalleled activity. I saw the much vaunted discoveries and inventions of by-gone days in their true proportions. They no longer preëmpted the whole world—present and future, as well as past, but, freed from romance, they ranged themselves in the form of a foundation upon which the structure of civilization is building. The successive steps in human achievement, from the use of fire to the harnessing of electricity, constituted a process of evolution creating "a stage where every man must play his part"—a part expanding and broadening with each succeeding generation; and I saw that I had a place among the actors in this play of progress. The forward steps of the past need not, and would not prevent me from achieving in the present—nay, they might even make a place, if I could but find it, for my feet; they might hold up my hands, and place within my grasp the keen tools with which I should do my work.

The school boy, passing from an attitude of contemplation and wonder before the things of the past into an attitude of active recognition of the necessities of the present, passed through the evolutionary process of the race. The savage, Sir Henry Maine tells us, lives in a state of abject fear, bound hand and foot by the sayings and doings of his ancestors and blinded by the terrors of nature. The lightning flashes, and the untutored mind, trembling, bows before the wrath of a jealous God; the harvest fails, and the savage humbly submits to the vengeance of an incensed deity; pestilence destroys the people, and the primitive man sees in this catastrophe a punishment inflicted on him for his failure to propitiate an exacting spirit—in these and a thousand other ways uncivilized peoples accept the phenomena in which nature displays her power, as the expressed will of an omnipotent being. One course alone is open to them; they must bow down before the unknown, accepting as inevitable those forces which they neither can understand nor conquer.

Civilization has meant enlightenment and achievement. In lightning, Franklin saw a potent giant which he enslaved for the service of man; in famine, Burbank discovered a lack of proper adjustment between the soil and the crops that men were cultivating—thereupon he produced a wheat that would thrive on an annual rainfall of twelve inches; in pestilence, Pasteur recognized the ravages of an organism which he prepared to study and destroy. Lightning, famine and pestilence are, to the primitive man, the threatening of a wrathful god; but to the progressive thinker they are merely forces which must be utilized or counteracted in the work of human achievement.

As a boy, I believed my opportunities to be limited by the achievements of the past. As a man, I see in these past achievements not hindrances, but the foundation stones which the past has laid down, upon which the present must build, in order that the future may erect the perfected structure of a higher civilization. I see all of this clearly, and I see one thing more. In the old days which I had erstwhile envied, one event of world import might have been chronicled for each decade, but in the nineteenth and twentieth centuries, such an event may be chronicled for each year, or month or even for each day. The achievements of the past were noteworthy: these of the present are stupendous.

The process of social evolution reveals itself in these progressive steps. Because the past has built, the present is building—building in order that the future may stand higher in its realization of potential life. The past was an age of uncertain, hesitating advance. The present, an age of dynamic achievement, leads on into the future of human development.

In the twentieth century:

1. Knowledge provides a basis for activity.

2. The social atmosphere palpitates with enthusiastic resolve and abounds in noble endeavor.

3. There is work for each one to perform.

The despondent boy has thus evolved into the enthusiastic worker whose watchword is "Forward!"—forward towards a new goal, whose very existence is made attainable through the achievements of the past: a goal before which the triumphs of bygone ages pale into insignificance.

The past worked with things. Pyramids were built, cities constructed, mountains tunneled, trade augmented, fortunes amassed. Hear Ruskin's comment on this devotion to material wealth: "Nevertheless, it is open, I repeat, to serious question, ... whether, among national manufactures, that of souls of a good quality may not at last turn out a quite lucrative one. Nay, in some far-away and yet undreamed of hour, I can even imagine that England ... as a Christian mother, may at last attain to the virtues and the treasures of a heathen one, and be able to lead forth her sons, saying: 'These are my jewels.'"[1]

The past worked with things: the future, rising higher in the scale of civilization, must work with men—with the plastic, living clay of humanity. As Solomon long ago said, "He that ruleth his own spirit is greater than he that taketh a city." The men of the past built cities and took them. They brought the forces of nature into subjection and remodeled the world as a living place for humanity, yet, save for a shadow in Rome and an echo from Greece, there is scarcely a trace in history of a consistent attempt to evolve nobler men.

Material objects have cost the nations untold effort, but human fiber—the life blood of nations—has been overlooked or forgotten. The world is weary of this emphasis on things and this forgetfulness of men; the ether trembles with the clamor for manhood. The fields, white to harvest, are awaiting the laborers who, building on the discoveries and inventions of things in the past, will so mold the human clay of the present that the future may boast a society of men and women possessing the qualities of the Super Race.

What is a Super Race? Nothing more nor less than a race representing, in the aggregate, the qualities of the Super Man—the qualities which enable one possessing them to live what Herbert Spencer described so luminously as a "complete life," namely,—

    1. Physical normality.
    2. Mental capacity.
    3. Concentration.
    4. Aggressiveness.
    5. Sympathy.
    6. Vision.

These characteristics of the Super Man express themselves in his activity:

    1. Physical normality provides energy.
    2. Mental capacity gives mental grasp.
    3. Aggressiveness. }
    }produce efficiency.
    4. Concentration. }
    5. Sympathy leads to harmony with things and

coöperation with men.

6. Vision shows itself in ideals.

The energy to do; and the mental grasp to appreciate; together with the capacity to choose efficiently, furnish the basis for achievement. Achievement, however, is not in itself a guarantee of worth unless its course is shaped by sympathy and directed toward a goal which is determined by the prophetic power of vision. Such are the characteristics which, combined in one individual, insure completeness of life. About them, philosophers have reasoned and poets have sung. They are the acme of human perfection—the ideal of individual attainment.

Though they have been thus idealized, these qualities are not new. They have existed for ages, as they exist to-day, occasionally combined in one individual but usually appearing separately in members of the social group. They form part of the heritage of the human race, and in spite of neglect and lack of fostering, they are widespread in all sections of the population. The production of a race of men and women, a great majority of whom shall possess these qualities, will mean the next great step in human achievement.

The Super Man has lived for ages. The Greeks traced the descent of their heroes and heroines—their Super Men—from the Gods. It was thus that they explained exceptional ability. Exceptional men live to-day, as they did in ancient Greece, directing the thought and work of the times. They possess the qualities of the Super Man—physical normality, mental capacity, aggressiveness, concentration, sympathy and vision; and, above all, we now understand that they are not the offspring of the gods, but the sons of men and women whose combined parental qualities inevitably produced Super Men. The Super Man is not a theory, nor an accident, but a natural product of natural conditions.

Though the Super Man may be met with occasionally in modern society, and though the qualities ascribed to him are manifest everywhere among those who have had an opportunity for their development; opinions still differ as to the possibility of producing a Super Race. An even greater difference of opinion is encountered when an attempt is made to formulate the means which should be adopted to secure such an end; yet there can be little difference of opinion as to the desirability, from a national as well as from an individual standpoint, of creating a race of Super Men.

The call of the present age for a Super Race is thus voiced by Yeats,[2]

> "O Silver Trumpets! Be you lifted up,
> And cry to the great race that is to come.
> Long throated swans, amid the Waves of Time,

> Sing loudly, for beyond the wall of the World
> It waits, and it may hear and come to us."

We long for the coming of the Super Race. We aim toward this goal. Can it be compassed in finite time? Is Nietzsche right when he says,—"I teach you beyond-man." "All beings hitherto have created something beyond themselves." "What is great in man is that he is a bridge and not a goal." "Not whence ye come, be your honor in the future, but whither ye go!" "In your children ye shall make amends for being your father's children. Thus ye shall redeem all that is past."[3]

Shall we make amends to the future? Come, then, let us reason together concerning the measures which must be adopted to raise the standard of succeeding generations. There are three means which lie ready at hand: three sciences which lend themselves to our task: three tools with which we may shape the Super Race. They are:

1. Eugenics—The science of race culture.

2. Social adjustment—The science of molding institutions.

3. Education—The science of individual development.

The science of Eugenics treats of those forces which, through the biologic processes of heredity, may be relied upon to provide the inherited qualities of the Super Race. The science of Social Adjustment treats of those forces which, through the modification of social institutions, may be relied upon to provide a congenial environment for the Super Race. The science of Education aims to assist the child in unfolding and developing the hereditary qualities of the Super Man, provided through eugenic guarantees. Hence, Eugenics, Social Adjustment and Education are sciences, the mastery of which is a pre-requisite to the development of the Super Race.

CHAPTER II
EUGENICS—THE SCIENCE OF RACE CULTURE

The object of Eugenics is the conscious improvement of the human race by the application of the laws of heredity to human mating. Eugenics is the logical fruition of the progress in biologic science made during the nineteenth century.

The laws of heredity, studied in minute detail, have been applied with marvelous success in the vegetable and animal kingdoms. "Is there any good reason," demands the eugenist, "why the formulas which have operated to re-combine the physical properties of plants and animals, should not in like measure operate to modify the physical properties of men and women?"

The studies which have been made of eye color, length of arm, head shape, and other physical traits show that the same laws of heredity which apply in the animal and vegetable kingdoms apply as well in the kingdom of man. Since the species of plants and animals with which man has experimented have been improved by selective breeding, there seems to be no good reason why the human race should not be susceptible of similar improvement. What intelligent farmer sows blighted potatoes? Where is the dog fancier who would strive to rear a St. Bernard from a mongrel dam? Neither yesterday nor yet to-morrow do men gather grapes of thorns. Those who have to do with life in any form, aware of this fact, refuse to permit propagation except among the best members of a species: hence with each succeeding generation the ox increases in size and strength; the apple in color; the sweet pea in perfume; and the horse in speed. Is this law of improving species a universal law? Alas, no! it rarely if ever applies in the selection of men and women for parenthood. The human species has not, during historic times, improved either in physique, in mental capacity, in aggressiveness, in concentration, in sympathy or in vision. Nay, there are not wanting thoughtful students who affirm that in almost every one of these respects the exact contrary holds true.

There appears to be some question as to whether the best of the Greek athletes exceeded in strength and skill the modern professional athlete, but there is no doubt at all that the average citizen of Athens was a more perfect specimen physically than the average citizen of twentieth century America.

Some students insist that the level of intellectual capacity has been raised, yet Galton, after a careful survey of the field, concludes in his *Hereditary Genius* that the average citizen of Athens was at least two degrees higher in the scale of intellectual attainment than the average Englishman; Carl Snyder[4] boldly maintains that the intellectual ability of scientific men is less to-day than it was in past centuries; while Mrs. Martin,[5] in a study more novel than scientific, insists that the genius of the modern world is on a level distinctly below that of the genius of Greece.

Perhaps American commercial aggressiveness is equal to the military aggressiveness of the Romans, the early Germans, and the followers of Attila. We have concentrated most of our efforts upon industry, yet even here, our concentration is no greater than that of the poets of the Elizabethan era, or the religious zealots of the Middle Ages. Our sympathy with beauty is at so low an ebb that we fail even to approach the standard of past ages. Neither in art, in sculpture, nor in poetry do our achievements compare with those of the earlier Mediterranean civilizations; while our knowledge of men as revealed in our literature is not above that of the Romans or the Athenians. As for vision, we still accept and strive to fulfill the commandments of the Prophet of Nazareth. In all of these fields, twentieth century America is equaled, if not outdone by the past.

Thus the distinctive qualities of the Super Man appear in the past with an intensity equal if not superior to that of the present. History records the transmutation of vegetable and animal species, the revolution of industry, the modification of social institutions, and the transformation of governmental systems; but in all historic time, it affirms no perceptible improvement in the qualities of man. "We must replace the man by the Super Man," writes G. Bernard Shaw.[6] "It is frightful for the citizen, as the years pass him, to see his own contemporaries so exactly reproduced by the younger generation."

Nevertheless, the possibility of race improvement exists. "What now characterizes the exceptionally high may be expected eventually to characterize all, for that which the best human nature is capable of is within the reach of human nature at large."[7] After years of intensive study, Spencer thus confidently expressed himself. Since he ceased to work, each bit of scientific data along eugenic lines serves to confirm his opinion. Armed with such a belief and with the assurance which scientific research has afforded, we are preparing in this eleventh hour to fulfill Spencer's predictions.

There are two fields in which eugenics may be applied—the first, Negative, the second, Positive. Through the establishment of Negative Eugenics the unfit will be restrained from mating and perpetuating their unfitness in the future. Through Positive Eugenics the fit may be induced to mate, and by combining their fitness in their offspring, to raise up each new generation out of the flower of the old. Negative Eugenics eliminates the unfit; Positive Eugenics perpetuates the fit.

The field of Negative Eugenics has been well explored. No question exists as to the transmission through heredity of feeble mindedness, idiocy, insanity and certain forms of criminality. "There is one way, only one way, out of this difficulty. Modern society ... must declare that there shall be no unfit and defective citizens in the State."[8] The Greeks eliminated unfitness by the destruction of defective children; though we may deplore such a practice in the light of our modern ethical codes, we recognize the end as one essential to race progress. By denying the right of parenthood to any who have transmissible disease or defect, our modern knowledge enables us to accomplish the same end without recourse to the destruction of human life.

Sir Francis Galton, the founder of the science of Eugenics, writes, in his last important work, "I think that stern compulsion ought to be exerted to prevent the free propagation of the stock of those who are seriously afflicted by lunacy, feeble-mindedness, habitual criminality and pauperism."[9] Yet society, in dealing with hereditary defect, presents some of its most grotesque inconsistencies. "It is a curious comment on the artificiality of our social system that no stigma attaches to preventable ill-health." An empty purse, or a ruined home may mean social ostracism, but "break-down in person, whatever the cause, evokes sympathy, subscription and silence."[10]

Certain defects are known to be transmissible by heredity from parent to child, until the *crétin* of Balzac's *Country Doctor* is reproduced for centuries. The remedy for this form of social self-torture lies in the denial of parenthood to those who have transmissible defects. Individually, such a denial works hardships in this generation: socially, and to the future generations, it means comparative freedom from individual, and hence from social defect.

The problem of Positive Eugenics presents an essentially different aspect. As Ruskin so well observes—"It is a matter of no final concern, to any parent, whether he shall have two children or four; but matter of quite final concern whether those he has shall or shall not deserve to be hanged." The quality is always the significant factor. Whether in family or national progress, an effort must be made to insure against hanging, or against any tendency that leads gallowsward.

Positive Eugenics is the science of race building through wise mating. "As long as ability marries ability, a large proportion of able offspring is a certainty."[11] What prospective parent does not fondly imagine that his children will be at least near-great? Yet how many individuals, in their choice of a mate, set out with the deliberate intention of securing a life partner whose qualities, when combined with his own, must produce greatness?

The Darwin-Galton-Wedgwood families boast sixteen men of world fame in five generations; in the Bach family there were fifty-seven musicians of note in eight generations; Wood's study of *Heredity in Royalty* shows the evident transmission of special ability; yet men and women of ability, anxious for able offspring, mate without any rational effort to secure the end which they desire. "Ninety-nine times out of a hundred our mathematician marries a woman whose family did not count a single astronomer, physicist or other mathematical mind among it members. The result of such a union is what could be expected. Although genius does not generally die out right away in the first generation, it decreases by half, and further dilutions soon bring it down to nothingness."[12]

This, in brief, is the problem of Negative and of Positive Eugenics. Both defect and ability are transmitted by heredity; both are the product of the mating process known as marriage; since society can and does control marriage, it may, through this control, exercise a real influence upon the character of future generations.

The science of Eugenics is in its infancy, yet, widely established and vigorously applied, it may revolutionize the human species. The Super Race may come, because "looked at from the social standpoint, we see how exceptional families, by careful marriages, can within even a few generations, obtain an exceptional stock, and how directly this suggests assortative mating as a moral duty for the highly endowed. On the other hand, the exceptionally degenerate isolated in the slums of our modern cities can easily produce permanent stock also: a stock which no change of environment will permanently elevate, and which nothing but mixture with better blood will improve. But this is an improvement of the bad by a social waste of the better. We do not want to eliminate bad stock by watering it with good, but by placing it under conditions where it is relatively or absolutely infertile."[13]

"But what of love?" wails the sentimentalist; "in your scheme Eugenics outweighs Cupid!" Perhaps, but what of it? Cupid has proved in the past a sad bungler, whose mistakes and failures grimace from every page of our divorce court records. Far from hindering his activities, however, Eugenics will assist Cupid by bringing together persons truly congenial—hence capable of an enduring love. Too many men have married a natty Easter bonnet, or a cleverly tailored suit. Too many women have fallen a prey to a tempting bank account or a pair of glorious mustachios. Blind Cupid limps but lamely over the rugged path of matrimonial bliss. The questionable success of his best efforts proves his sure need of a guide.

Eugenics represents an effort to bring together those people who have complementary qualities and complementary interests; who are capable of maintaining congenial relationships in the present; and creating able offspring in the future. Selection and parenthood are the cradle of the future. Hence the individual who, in the exercise of his choice, overlooks their significance overlooks one of his most important racial responsibilities.

Society is interested in Eugenics, because it is through Eugenics that the hereditary traits of the Super Race are perpetuated and perfected. Eugenics, rightly understood and applied, is a social asset of unexcelled value. How long, then, shall our society continue to feed on the husks, neglecting the grain which lies everywhere ready at hand?

Eugenics is indeed one means of race salvation, yet what care do we take to perfect eugenic measures? "If through sheer chance, some great mathematician is evolved one day out of the crowd, the state—who should be ever on the watch for such events and whose main care should be to preserve and increase such sources of light, progress and national glory—does nothing to protect the man of genius against care, disease or anything likely to shorten life nor to multiply the splendid thinking machine."[14] A great state must have for its component parts great men and women. Did we truly seek greatness, how many measures for its attainment lie neglected at our very doors!

Every well regulated state of antiquity eliminated defectives in the interest of the group, and of the future. What more effective means of social preservation could be imagined than some measure through whose operation the defective classes in society would be eliminated, and the social structure, bulwarked by stalwart manhood and womanhood, made proof against the ravages of time. How serious a thing is the propagation of defect! Murder is a crime, punishable by death, yet a murderer merely eliminates one unit from the social group. The destruction of this one life may cause sorrow; it may deprive society of a valued member; but it is, after all, a comparatively insignificant offense. The perpetuation of hereditary defect is infinitely worse than murder. Consider, for example, a marriage, sanctioned by church and state, between two persons both having in their blood hereditary feeble-mindedness.

Investigations of thousands of feeble-minded families show that, in such a case, every one of the offspring may be and probably will be feeble-minded—a curse to himself and a burden to society. Pauperism, crime, social dependence, vice, all follow in the train of mental defect, and the mentally defective parents hand on for untold generations their taint—sometimes in more, sometimes in less virulent form, but always bringing into the world beings not only incapable of caring for themselves, but fatally capable of handing on their defect to the future. The murderer robs society; the mentally defective parent curses society, both in the present and in the future, with the taint of degeneracy. The murderer takes away a life; but the feeble-minded parent passes on to the future the seeds of racial decay.

The first step in Eugenics progress—the elimination of defect by preventing the procreation of defectives—is easily stated, and may be almost as easily attained. The price of six battleships ($50,000,000) would probably provide homes for all of the seriously defective men, women and children now at large in the United States. Thus could the scum of society be removed, and a source of social contamination be effectively regulated. Yet with tens of thousands of defectives, freely propagating their kind, we continue to build battleships, fondly believing that rifled cannon and steel armor plate will prove sufficient for national defense.

This is but a part, and by far the least important part, of the eugenic programme. The elimination of defect prevents degeneracy, but does not insure the physical normality, mental capacity, aggressiveness, concentration, sympathy and vision of the Super Man. While the elimination of defect is imperative, it is after all only the first step toward the creation of positive qualities.

Positive Eugenics may be as obvious as Negative Eugenics, but the promulgation of its doctrines is not equally easy. A series of legislative enactments will prevent the mating of the hereditarily defective; nothing but the most painstaking education can be relied upon to secure the mating of those eugenically fit. Nevertheless for that modern state which seeks to persist and dominate, no lesser measure will suffice. After all, why should not society educate its youth to a sense of wisdom in mating? The United States spends each year some four hundred millions of dollars in public education, teaching children to read, to spell, to sew, to draw. The importance of these studies is obvious, yet, from a social standpoint, they cannot compare in significance with such training in the laws of heredity and biology as will insure wise choice in mating. The state, in its efforts at self preservation, cannot lay too much emphasis on the training for eugenic choice.

Biology, through the laws of heredity, applied in the science of Eugenics, holds out every hope for the coming of the Super Man and of the Super

Race. Not in our knowledge of its laws, but in the practice of its precepts, are we lacking.

Eugenics, it is true, in its negative and positive phases, holds out a great hope for the future. But Eugenics alone will not suffice. The science of Eugenics must be coupled with the science of Social Adjustment to insure the production of a Super Race. The necessity of this union is well recognized by the students of heredity, while the students of Social Adjustment found their theories on premises essentially biologic in origin. One of the most widely known writers on heredity concludes a recent book with the statement that—"At present, we can only indicate that the future of our race depends on Eugenics (in some form or other), combined with the simultaneous evolution of eutechnics and eutopias. 'Brave words,' of course; but surely not 'Eutopian'!"[15] Thus the knowledge and practice of the laws of heredity must be supplemented by a knowledge and practice of the laws of Social Adjustment.

CHAPTER III
SOCIAL ADJUSTMENT—THE SCIENCE OF MOLDING INSTITUTIONS

After a gardener has produced his seed, guaranteeing a good heredity by breeding together those individual plants which possess in the highest degree the qualities he desires to secure, he turns his attention to the seed bed. First of all, the location must be good—the bed must be on a southern slope, where it will benefit by the first warm rays of the spring sun; then the soil must be finely pulverized, in order that the tiny rootlets may easily force their way downward, finding nourishment ready at hand; when the seeds have been planted, in ground well prepared and fertilized, they must be watered, cultivated, weeded; and as they develop into larger plants, thinned, transplanted, pruned and sprayed. The wise gardener considers environment as well as heredity. By sowing choice seeds in well prepared soil, he ensures the excellence of his crop.

Modern society may well be compared to a garden. The plants are living, moving beings, with some freedom to act on their own initiative. Moreover, it is they who make and tend the gardens in which they grow. Like the gardener in the story, they must look to environment as well as to heredity. The seed bed must be carefully prepared, and the young plants, as they appear, must be given all the attention which science makes possible. Modern society is a garden of which the products are men and women. The sowing, weeding, cultivating—carried forward through social institutions—determines by its character whether the race shall decay, as other races have done, or progress toward the Super Man.

The science of social gardening—Social Adjustment—has been given a great impetus, in recent years, by the increased knowledge of the relative influences of heredity and environment in determining the status of the individual. This knowledge has led us to a belief in men.

Earlier beliefs conceived of the majority of men as utterly depraved. Some indeed were among the elect, but the remainder, born to the lowest depths of the social gehenna, were outcasts and pariahs, helpless in this world and hopeless in the next. This doctrine of total depravity set at nought all progressive effort. Here stands a man—society has called him a criminal. Last year he attempted to steal an automobile, less than three weeks after his release from serving a two-year sentence for grand larceny. To-day he is in court again, charged with entering a lodging house and stealing three pairs of trousers and an overcoat. The man is on trial for burglary—what shall be the social verdict regarding him?

"Alas," mourns the advocate of total depravity, "God so made him. It is not our right to interfere."

"Wait," says the social scientist, "until I investigate the case."

The case is held over while the scientist makes his investigation. After careful inquiry, he reports that the young man's criminal record began at the age of nine, when he was arrested for stealing bananas from a freight car. Locked up with older criminals, he soon learned their tricks. He was "nimble" and could "handle himself," so his prison mates taught him the science of pocket picking, and initiated him into the gentle art of "shop lifting." He was released, after two months of this schooling, and slipping out into the big, black city, he tried an experiment. Succeeding, he tried again, and yet again. Before the month was out, he was detected stealing a silk handkerchief, and was back in prison. There his education was perfected, and he entered the world to try once more. From the world to jail, from jail to the world—this boy's life history from the age of nine, had been one long attempt to learn his trade; fortunately or unfortunately, he was somewhat of a bungler, and sooner or later he was always caught.

When he was a boy, he sneaked up a dingy court, and three pairs of dirty stairs to a landing where, in the rear of a battered tenement, was an abode which he had been taught to call home. His father, a dock laborer, earned, on the average, about $300 a year. Sometimes he worked steadily, day and night, for a week, and earned $25 or $30; then there would be no work for ten days or perhaps two weeks; the money would run out; the grocer would refuse credit; and the family would be hungry. It was during one of these hungry intervals that the nine-year-old urchin made his descent on the bananas in the freight car, and received his first jail sentence.

His mother, good hearted but woefully ignorant, made the best of things, taking in washing, doing odd jobs here and there, tending to her children, when opportunity offered, and at other times letting them run the streets.

"There," concludes the social scientist, "is the story of that boy's life. His only picture of manhood is an inefficient father who cannot earn enough to support his family; his concept of a mother expresses itself in good hearted ignorance; his view of society has been secured from the rear of a shabby tenement, the curb of a narrow street and a cell in the county jail. The seed bed has been neither prepared, watered, nor tended, and the young shoot has grown wild."

The social scientist has not been content with an analysis of social maladjustment; going further, he has transplanted the young shoots from the defective seed bed to better ground. Dr. Bernardo organized a system for taking the boy criminals out of the slums of English cities, and sending them to farms in Australia, South Africa and Canada. Nearly 50,000 boys have been thus disposed of. Though in their home cities many of them had already entered a criminal life, in their new surroundings less than two per cent. of them showed any tendency to revert to their former criminal practices. A little tending and transplanting into a congenial environment, proved the salvation of these boys, who would otherwise have thronged the jails of England.

Careful analysis has convinced the social scientist that, in the absence of malformation of the brain, or of some other physical defect, the average man is largely made by his environment. As serious physical defect is quite rare, being present in less than five per cent. of the population; and as only a small percentage of the population, perhaps two or three per cent., is above the average in ability, more than nine-tenths of the people remain average—shaped by their environment; capable of good or of evil, according as the good or evil forces of society influence their youth and early maturity.

The eighteenth century philosophers had embodied the same conclusion in the doctrine that all men are created free and equal. Victor Hugo, in the first half of the nineteenth century, based most of his inspiring novels on the theory that in every man there is a divine spark—a conscience—which will be developed by a good environment or crushed and blackened by a bad one.

Each year added new proofs of the theory of universal capacity, until Ward was able to write his *Applied Sociology*, demonstrating that opportunity is the key-note of social progress.[16] For, says he, up to the present time nine-tenths of the men, and ten-tenths of the women (nineteen twentieths of society) have been denied a legitimate opportunity for development. Grant this opportunity, and at once, without any change in hereditary characteristics, you can increase, nineteen fold, the achievements of society.

Ward's estimate may be or may not be exactly correct. His contention that universalized opportunity would greatly augment social achievement is, however, fundamentally sound. Social Adjustment aims, through the shaping social institutions, to provide every individual with an opportunity to secure a strong body, a trained mind, an aggressive attitude, the power of concentration, and the vision of a goal toward which he is working.[17] In short, the object of Social Adjustment is the provision of universal opportunity.

The dark unfathomed caves of ocean bear many a gem of purest ray serene. Even the most gifted individual, thrown into an adverse environment, will either fail utterly to develop his powers, or else will develop them so incompletely that they can never come to their full fruition. Thomas A. Edison cast away on an island in the South Pacific would be useless to his fellows. Abraham Lincoln, living among the Apache Indians, would have left small impress on the world. A sculptor, to be really great, must go to Rome, because it is in Rome that the great works of sculptured art are to be found. It is in Rome, furthermore, that the great sculptors work and teach. A lawyer can scarcely achieve distinction while practicing in a backwoods county court, nor can a surgeon remain proficient in his science unless he keep in constant touch with the world of surgery. "I must go to the city," cried a woman with an unusual voice. "Here in the country I can sing, but I cannot study music." She must, of necessity, go to the city because in the city alone exists the stimulus and the example which are necessary for the perfection of her art.

A congenial environment is necessary for the perfection of any hereditary talent. Lester F. Ward concludes, after an exhaustive analysis of self-made men, that such men are the exception. That they exist he must admit, but that their abilities would have come to a much more complete development in a congenial environment he clearly demonstrates.

The rigorous persecution of the Middle Ages eliminated any save the most daring thinkers. Men of science, who presumed to assert facts in contradiction of the accepted dogmas of the Church, were ruthlessly silenced, hence the ages were very dark. The nineteenth century, on the contrary, through its cultivation of science and scientific attainments, has reaped a harvest of scientific achievement unparalleled in the history of the world. Men to-day enter scientific pursuits for the same reason that they formerly entered the military service—because every emphasis is laid on scientific endeavor. The nineteenth century scientist is the logical outcome of the nineteenth century desires for scientific progress.

The environment shapes the man. Yet, equally, does the man shape the environment. A high standard individual may be handicapped by social tradition, but, in like manner, progressive social institutions are inconceivable in the absence of high standard men and women.

The institutions of a society—its homes, schools, government, industry—are created by the past and shaped by the present. Institutions are not subjected to sudden changes, yet one generation, animated by the effort to realize a high ideal, may reshape the social structure.

Can one conceive of a paper strewn campus in a college where the spirit is strong? Parisians believe in beauty, hence Paris is beautiful. Social institutions combine the achievements of the past with the ethics of the present.

"Let me see where you live and I will tell you what you are," is a true saying. The social environment, moldable in each generation, is an accurate index to the ideals and aspirations of the generation in which it exists.

CHAPTER IV
EDUCATION—THE SCIENCE OF INDIVIDUAL DEVELOPMENT

Eugenics provides the hereditary qualities of the Super Man; Social Adjustment furnishes the environment in which these qualities are to develop; there still remains the development of the individual through Education, a word which means, for our purposes, all phases of character shaping from birth-day to death-day.

The individual has been rediscovered during the past three centuries. He was known in some of the earlier civilizations, but during the Middle Ages the place that had seen him knew him no more. He was submerged in the group and forced to subordinate his interests to the demands of group welfare. The distinctive work of the eighteenth and nineteenth centuries has been a reversal of this enforced individual oblivion and the formulation of a demand for individual initiative and activity. The individual, pushed forward in politics, in religion, and in commerce has freely asserted and successfully maintained his right to consideration, until the opportunities of the twentieth century free citizen far exceed those of the convention-bound citizen of the middle ages. The twentieth century citizen is free because he makes efficient choices. The continuance of his freedom depends upon the continued wisdom of his choice.

The chief objective point of modern endeavor has been individual freedom of choice. The *laissez-faire* doctrine in commercial relations, democracy in politics, the natural philosophy and natural theology of the eighteenth century are all expressions of a belief in equality. When men are made free to choose, they are placed on a basis of equality, since they have a like opportunity to succeed or fail. The man who chooses rightly wins success—the man who chooses wrongly fails.

Thus the freedom to choose is for the average man a right of inestimable value, because it places in his hands the opportunity to achieve. Rights do not, however, come alone. The freeman is bound in his choices to recognize the law that rights are always accompanied by duties.

Each right is accompanied by a proportionate responsibility—there is no dinner without its dishwashing. To be sure, you may shift the burden of dishwashing to the maid, and the burden of voting to the "other fellow," but the responsibility is none the less present. Garbage is still garbage, even when thrown into the well, and your responsibilities, shifted to the maid and the other voter, return to plague you in the form of a servant problem and of vicious politics. Men who have a right to choose have also a duty to fulfill, and this right and this duty are inseparable.

The eighteenth century began the discovery of the individual man; the nineteenth century—at least the latter half of it—was responsible for the discovery of the individual woman. Even to-day in many civilized lands, the woman is merely an appendage. Men innumerable write in the hotel register "John Edwards and Wife," yet if the truth were told they should often write "Jane Edwards and John Edwards," and perhaps sometimes "Jane Edwards and husband."

Western civilization, a good unthinking creature, has insisted bravely on the development of the individual man, while largely overlooking the existence of the individual woman; yet the studies of heredity show very clearly that at least as many qualities are inherited from the female as from the male. Nay, further, since the female is less specialized, the distinctive race qualities are inherited from her, rather than from the more specialized male. In short, the Super Man will have a mother as well as a father.

The fact that the average man has as many female as he had male ancestors is very frequently overlooked. Yet it is a fact that inevitably carries with it the imputation, that if his ancestors were thus equally apportioned, he must have inherited his qualities from both sexes. Therefore, in the production of the Super Man, the qualities of the woman are of equal importance with the qualities of the man.

The individual is the goal and Education the means, since Education is the science of individual development. Through Education, we shall enable the individual to live completely. But what is complete life? How shall we compass or define it?

Two laws are laid down as fundamental in nature—the laws of self preservation and of self perpetuation. With the development of society, and social relations, the individual must recognize himself, not as an individual only, but likewise as a unit in a social group. Hence, for him, self preservation and self perpetuation necessarily involve group preservation and group perpetuation. His code of life must therefore formulate itself in this wise—

THE OBJECTS OF ENDEAVOR

	Immediate	*Ultimate*
INDIVIDUAL	Self Expression	Super Man

SOCIAL {
Eugenics
Social Adjustment   Super Race
Education

The individual, for self preservation, demands self expression; for self perpetuation he demands that the standard of his children be higher than his own. As a member of the social group, he looks to Eugenics, Social Adjustment, and Education as the immediate means of raising social standards, and the ultimate means of providing a Super Race.

Such are the abstract ideals—how may they be practically applied? How shall the individual express, through Eugenics, Social Adjustment, and Education his desire for the development of a Super Race?

Do you, sir, enjoy living in the neighborhood of vandals and thieves? Well, hardly. One could not be expected to take so frivolous a view of life, therefore you will in self defense take every possible precaution to suppress vandalism and thievery? Never, my dear sir, never! You must take every possible precaution to reduce the spirit of vandalism and of thievery. The acts are in themselves unconsequential—they are but the product of a diseased mind or an indifferent training. The spirit, here as elsewhere, is all important.

Are you a scientist? Do you admire Pasteur and Herbert Spencer? You are a "practical" man—see what Edison has done for you. As a statesman, you revere Lincoln and Daniel Webster. You cannot, as an artist, overlook the portraits of Rembrandt or the water scenes of Ruysdael. You must agree with me that these and a thousand others that I might mention—men called geniuses by their contemporaries or their descendants—have contributed untold worth to the society of which they were a part. They chose rightly. They are looked upon, and justly, as the salt of the earth. You admit the value of geniuses, in civilization, and you would, of course, do anything to increase their number? Then, let me say to you that the first thing for you to decide is that your own children shall be neither vandals nor thieves. The second thing for you to decide is that they shall, in so far as you are able to determine the matter, possess all of your good qualities, coupled with the good qualities which you lack, supplied by an able mate. In short, you must choose your life partner with a view to the elimination of anti-social tendencies, on the one hand, and on the other to the development of the qualities which distinguish the Super Man.

How obvious is this statement, yet how haphazard has been the production of greatness. Only once in a generation does a man, in his choice of a wife, follow the example of John Newcomb. In a truly scientific spirit he enumerated on paper the qualities which he possessed; placed opposite them the qualities in which he was lacking; and then set out to find the woman who should supply his deficiencies. When he had located his future helpmeet, playing hymn tunes on an organ in a little red school house, and upon further acquaintance, had assured himself that she really possessed the needed qualities, he married her, with the determination that their first child should be a great mathematician. Their first child was Simon Newcomb, one of the leading astronomers of the nineteenth century.

John Newcomb was a village school master, and his wife a village maiden, but in their choice they combined two sets of qualities which would inevitably produce a Super Man. John Newcomb was a pioneer eugenist. He chose a mate with the thought of the future foremost in his mind.

Too often, however, the men of parts follow the example of the brilliant professor who married a "social butterfly." "Why in the world did you do it?" asked an old friend. "Oh, well," answered the professor, "I felt that I had brains enough for both."

True, professor, but according to the Mendelian law of heredity, those brains of yours will be halved in each of your children, and quartered in each of your grandchildren. Why should not the future be at least as brilliant as your own generation?

Human marriage is ordinarily a hit or miss affair. Men and women, inspired by the loftiest motives, and animated in most matters by supreme good sense, not infrequently grope blindly toward matrimony; often marry uncongenially; and finally bring disgrace upon their own heads, and misery upon their families. Stevenson, with such marriages in mind, writes to the average prospective bridegroom—

"What! you have had one life to manage, and have failed so strangely, and now can see nothing wiser than to conjoin with it the management of some one else's? Because you have been unfaithful in a very little, you propose yourself to be a ruler over ten cities. You are no longer content to be your own enemy; you must be your wife's also. God made you, but you marry yourself; no one is responsible but you. You have eternally missed your way in life, with consequences that you still deplore, and yet you masterfully seize your wife's hand, and blindfold, drag her after you to ruin. And it is your wife, you observe, whom you select. She, whose happiness you most desire, you choose to be your victim. You would earnestly warn her from a tottering bridge or bad investment. If she were to marry some one else, how you would tremble for her fate! If she were only your sister and you thought half as much of her, how doubtfully would you entrust her future to a man no better than yourself!"[18]

Here, then, lies the path of eugenic activity for the individual—clear, straight, unmistakable. In the first place, he must never transmit to the future any defect. If he has a transmissible defect, he must have no offspring. This seems but reasonable—an obligation to bring no unnecessary misery into a world where so much already exists. But the individual—free to choose—must go one step further, and in his selection, must seek a mate with the qualities which are complementary to his own.

Looked at from the standpoint of society, there is no single choice which compares in importance to the choice of a mate; for on that choice depend the qualities which this generation will transmit to the next, and from which the next generation must create its follower. Furthermore, there is no choice which, in modern society, is more completely individual—more freed from social interference, than the choice of a life mate. The man in choosing his life partner, chooses the future. Civilization hangs expectant on his decision. The Super Race, dim and indistinct, may be made a living reality by a eugenic choice in the present—a choice for which each man and woman who marries is in part responsible. With the advance of woman's emancipation, with the increasing range of her activity, comes an ever increasing opportunity to exercise such a choice. She, as well as the man, may now assist in the determination of the future. She as well as the man may now be held accountable for the non-appearance of the Super Race.

Does the burden of Eugenic Choice rest heavily upon the shoulders of the individual? Does he hesitate to assume the responsibility of the future race? The burden of shaping Social Adjustments is no less onerous.

Briefly, then, what changes may the individual make in institutions to develop the qualities of the Super Man? The social institutions with which the average man comes into the most intimate contact are:

    1. The Home.
    2. The School.
    3. The Government.

The home as an institution must provide for the Super Man enough food, clothing and shelter to guarantee him a good physique; enough training in coöperation and mutual helpfulness to give him the vision of a Super Race; and a supply of enthusiasm sufficient to enable him to work with increasing energy for the fulfillment of those things in which he believes. In order that the home may supply these things, it must have an income sufficient to provide all of the necessaries and some of the comforts of life. It must further be dominated by a spirit of sympathetic democracy.

While the present system of wealth distribution is so grotesquely unscientific that men are forced to rear families on incomes that will not provide the necessaries, to say nothing of the comforts, of life, no true home can be established nor can a Super Race be produced. If the child is an asset to the state, the state should support the child, guaranteeing to it an income sufficient to provide for its material welfare.

Why prate of home virtue? Why discourse learnedly on the possibilities of a developed manhood to a father earning nine dollars a week? If you can guarantee such a man an income of three dollars a week for each child, in addition to the nine dollars for his wife and himself, you may well air your views regarding a Super Race; but until your lowest income is high enough to guarantee the necessaries of life to a family of five; or until the state guarantees an income to each child in its early life, "You may as well go stand upon the beach and bid the main flood bate his usual height," as to demand that a man, working for starvation wages, provide a home in which Super Men can be reared.

When income has been provided; when there is food for every mouth, warm clothing for every back, enough fuel for winter, and a few pennies each week for recreation, then indeed you may begin to speak in terms of social improvement. Then, and then only, you may tell the father and the mother that upon their efforts during the first seven years of their children's lives depends the attitude which those children will assume when they go out into the world; that the home in which tyranny is unknown, in which the family rules the family, will produce the noblest citizens for the noblest state; that the home is still the most fundamental institution in civilization, the conservator of our ideals, and visions of the better things that are to come in the future—these things you may say, emphasizing the fact, that without a well rounded home-training in youth, even the noblest talents cannot come to their full fruition.

The school is a specialized form of home. In early days, when life was simple, and specialization was unknown, education was given almost wholly in the home; but with the growth of specialized tasks, the home could no longer fulfill its function as educator and the school was introduced. Education, whether given in the home or in the school, has as its object a complete life. The purpose of education is to enable the pupil to live completely—to be a rounded being, in whatever station he may be called upon to fill.

Would you mold the school to fit the needs of the children? Then, the system of education must be so shaped that children are prepared to live their lives completely. They must understand themselves. "Know thyself" is a command worthy of their attention. The child's body, in the period of change from childhood to adulthood, is an organism of the most delicate nature, barely reaching adjustment under the most auspicious conditions, and more than frequently failing signally from a lack of knowledge, or from the absence of sympathetic understanding. The child—the father of the man—must be taught to appreciate the human machine of which he is given charge. It is in the school, with its corps of specialists, that this work can be most effectively done.

Then, one by one, the school may take up and foster the qualities of the Super Man. Physique must come first. It is blatant mockery to speak of educating minds that dwell in anæmic bodies. Every boy and girl has a right to a strong, well knit frame, and the school must teach the best methods of securing it. Mental grasp—the power to see and judge a situation or combination of facts, may also come through the school. In fact, the school course, as at present organized, aims to secure that and little else. As the science of education advances, the same material which now comprises the entire course will be taught in less time and in wiser ways, so that the child shall be free to learn some of those other things so important to his soul's welfare. Aggressiveness and concentration are methods rather than ends, and can be made a part of every game, every competition, and every study, so that the child absorbs them as he absorbs the atmosphere, without knowing that they become a part of his being. Whether the school can instill sympathy and inspire vision is a question that the future alone must decide. Both may be given by individual teachers, and both may be possible to the school, though, if the home is doing its work, these things will come more effectively there than through the school. Most or all of the essential qualities of the Super Man can and will come through a well organized and properly directed educational system.

The government—providing the machinery of state administration, furnishing the school, the playground, and the library; affording an opportunity for the exercise of citizenship and the expression of those advancing ideas which must gradually remold the social institutions of each age in response to the demands of the new generation—affords one of the most potent forces for the development of the Super Man.

The school is the big home; the government is the big school. The child leaves the home, and enters the school; leaves the school and enters the state. In the home he is acted upon; in the school he, himself, begins to act; but in the government he is the sole actor—he is the state. A home must be higher than the children; the school must be more advanced than the pupils; but the state reflects exactly the character of its citizens. It is in the state that the Super Man, crystallizing his convictions and beliefs into the form of legislative enactments, must prepare the way for the Super Race.

The Super Race is the produce of heredity, of social environment, and of individual development. Heredity supplies the raw material—the individual human being, while education and social environment, operating upon this raw stuff, determine the course of its development. Steel is not made from bee's wax, nor is the Super Man created out of a defective heredity. In like manner, since those who are in Rome do as the Romans do, the raw material, no matter what its quality, is shaped by its surroundings. The old saying "as the twig is bent, the tree's inclined," should be modified in this one particular—the force which bends the twig must continue in the tree, else the latter will turn and grow toward the sky.

The stock of the Super Man will be secured by the mating of persons possessing the Super-Race qualities; yet, reared in an unfavorable environment, these qualities cannot produce the highest result.

Neither biologic nor social forces are alone adequate to develop the Super Race. Physique, mental capacity, aggressiveness, concentration, sympathy and vision are the products of heredity, social environment and training. The system of human mating must be perfected and the status of social institutions must be raised in order that the individuals produced in each generation may attain an additional increment of the qualities which will, in the end, produce the Super Race.

CHAPTER V
THE AMERICAN OPPORTUNITY

Here, in brief compass, are laid down the general principles upon which a nation must rely for the raising of its standard of human excellence. In general, we are convinced that the Super Race is possible. Specifically—and here is the next point—there are more possibilities for the development of the Super Race in the United States to-day than there have been in any nation of the past; or than there are in any nation of the present. The Super Race is America's distinctive opportunity.

The factors which may play so significant a part in establishing a Super Race in the United States are here set down in an order which permits of sequential treatment—

1. Natural resources.
2. The stock of the dominant races.
3. Leisure.
4. The emancipation of women.
5. The abandonment of war.
6. A knowledge of race making.
7. A knowledge of Social Adjustment.
8. A widespread educational machinery.

Natural resources are an indispensable element in national progress. A congenial climate is a pre-requisite to social development. No permanently successful civilization can be erected on the shores of Hudson Bay, or in the torrid heat of the Amazon Valley. The temperate zones, with their variable climate, and their wide range of vegetable products, seem to provide the foundation for the successful civilizations of the immediate future. No less necessary to civilization are harbors for the maintenance of commerce; and an abundance of minerals, the sinews of industry; and most important of all, fertile agricultural land.

In its possession of these natural resources, the United States is unexcelled. Its climate, while generally temperate, varies sufficiently to give an excellent range of products; harbors and rivers are abundant; forests and minerals are scattered everywhere; and the agricultural land, rich and well watered, is as extensive and as potentially productive as any equivalent area in the world. So far as natural resources provide a basis for a Super Race, the United States occupies a position of almost unique prominence.

The stock of the dominant races may or may not be a cant phrase. Notwithstanding the effective work done by Ripley in his *Races of Europe*,[19] an impression still prevails that certain races are, from their racial characteristics, specially fitted to dominate others. Woodruff, in his *Expansion of Races*,[20] takes this view, strongly urging the claim of the northwestern European to the distinction of world ruler. Whether race be a matter of supreme or of little concern, in determining the development of a Super Race, the United States possesses an admirable blending of the western European peoples who now occupy the dominant position in the commercial and military affairs of the world. If racial stock be a matter of no importance, it requires no emphasis; if, on the other hand, it be a significant factor in the creation of the Super Race, then the United States holds an enviable position in its racial qualities.

Thus the raw materials of nation building—the natural resources and the racial qualities, are possessed by the United States in generous abundance. Has our use of them tended toward the development of the Super Race?

Leisure is an opportunity for the pursuit of a congenial avocation. It must be carefully differentiated from the idleness with which it is so often considered synonymous. Satan still finds mischief for idle hands. The man who idles in leisure time is as likely now as ever in the past to find himself breaking several of the commandments. Leisure merely provides an opportunity for free choice. Unwisely used, it leads to individual dissipation and social degeneracy. Wisely employed, it is a most important means for the promotion of social progress.

Most of the great things of the world have been done in leisure time. A poet cannot create, nor can a mechanic devise, if he is forced during twelve hours each day to struggle for the bare necessities of life. A study of the lives of those who have made notable achievements in art, science, literature, and diplomacy shows that they were free, for the most part, from the bread and butter struggle. They had estates, they were the recipients of pensions, but they did not submit to the soul-destroying monotony of repeating the same task endlessly through the long reaches of a twelve hour day.

Primitive society demands the service of even its immature members. Children are adults before their childhood is well begun. Civilization, recognizing the possibility of self preservation through lengthened youth, has said to the child "Play."

Long youth means long life. Play time—leisure—for the youth is the bone and sinew of a high standard maturity. Leisure in youth for play, leisure in mature life for reflection and creation—these are two of the most precious gifts of civilization to social progress.

The United States has led the nations in providing opportunity for leisure time. Labor saving devices have been brought to a higher perfection there than in any other part of the world. Nowhere are children kept longer from assuming the responsibilities of adult life; in few countries is the workday shorter for adults.

Probably no other people in the world can supply themselves with the necessaries of life in so short a working time as can the inhabitants of the United States. If every able bodied adult engaged for five hours each day in gainful activity, enough economic goods could be created to provide all the necessaries and many of the comforts of life. The leisure obtained through American industry, if rightly directed, may provide for every child born a thorough education—an ample opportunity to express the qualities which are latent in him—and a thorough preparation for life.

The emancipation of women is another force which may be directed toward the improvement of race qualities. Women bear the race in their bodies; at least half of the qualities of the offspring are inherited from them; as mothers, they educate the children during the first six years of their lives, and then, as school teachers and mothers they play the leading part in education until the children reach the age of twelve or fourteen. The youth of the race is in women's keeping. They shape the child clay. The twig is bent, the tree is inclined by women's hands.

The emancipation of woman means her individualization. Both in primitive custom and in early law her individuality is merged in that of the man. "Wives," wrote Paul, "be obedient unto your husbands, for this is the law." Mohammedan women wear veils that they may not be seen; Chinese women bind their feet that they may not escape; the women of continental Europe spend their lives in ministering to the comfort of their liege lords. They are dependent—almost abject. From such a sowing, what must be the reaping? Into the hands of these subject creatures, men have committed the training of their sons.

Can a corrupt tree bring forth good fruit? If women are inferior to men, can they be worthy to train their future superiors—their sons? If they are of a lower mentality than men, how is it that, in the school as well as in the home, men have given into their hands the power to shape the destinies of the race?

Would you have your sons trained by a free man or by a slave? Do noble civic ideals flow from a citizen of a free commonwealth, or from the subjects of a despot? Only the woman who is a human being, with power and freedom to choose, may teach the son of a free man. Emancipation has given to women the power of choice.

The women of America have been partially emancipated. In some states, they may vote, sue for divorce, collect their own wages, hold property, and transact business. Everywhere they are filling the high schools and colleges; participating in industry and entering the professions. American women are independent beings—distinctive units in a great organic society.

In so far as the qualities of the Super Man are developed and perfected by the teachings of women, they will be more effectually rounded by the emancipated woman than by the serf. The mothers of America are prepared to teach their sons and daughters because they have been taught to think the noblest thoughts and do the strongest things.

The abandonment of war removes one of the most destructive forces of the past, because war has always tended to eliminate the best of every race. In the flower of their manhood, the noblest died on the field of battle—their lives uncompleted; their tasks unfinished—leaving, perhaps, no offspring to bear their qualities in the succeeding generation. Although the law of nature is the survival of the fittest, "In the red field of human history the natural process of selection is often reversed."[21] The best perish in war, leaving the less fit to carry forward the affairs of state, and to propagate. "The man who is left holds in his grasp the history of the future,"[22] and if, as is frequently the case, he is the one least fitted to survive, the race is constantly breeding from the unfit rather than from the fit. Where the human harvest is bad, the nation must perish. So long as war persisted, so long as the best left their bones on the battle field, while the worst left their descendants to man the state, a bad human harvest was inevitable. War ate into the heart of national vitality by destroying the nation's best blood.

War, however, has practically ceased. The movement for peace, in which the United States, both by precept and practice, is a leader, stands as one of the signal achievements of the new century. The abandonment of war has laid a basis for the Super Race by permitting the most fit to live and to hand on their special qualities to coming generations.

In the United States, as elsewhere in the civilized world, the science of race making has recently undergone great development. While the movement began in England, it has spread rapidly, until at the present time its significance is universally recognized by scientists. The principles of artificial selection have been applied in the creation of vegetable and animal prodigies; the knowledge of biologic and selective principles is wide-spread; and the educated men and women of the United States generally understand the potency of these forces.

Important steps have already been taken to prevent the propagation of the unfit. Born criminals are in some states deprived of the power of reproduction; in most of the states, the marriage of diseased persons is prohibited; here and there attempts have been made to prohibit the marriage of any suffering from a transmissible defect. On the other hand, mentally defective persons are being segregated in institutions—guarded against the dangers which beset the men and particularly the women of weak mind. During the past two decades great strides have been made in educating the American public to a higher standard of health and efficiency. Though the science of race making, as such, has not been given a prominent place in public discussion, the principles on which race making is based have formed an important element in public education. The desire to make a Super Race in America is as yet in its infancy, but the ground has been thoroughly prepared, and a foundation laid upon which such a superstructure of desire for race making can be speedily and effectively erected.

Meanwhile, the science of Social Adjustment has occupied the most prominent place in American thought. If the American people have under-emphasized Eugenics they have over-emphasized Social Adjustment. From ocean to ocean, the country has been swept, during the past three decades, by a whirlwind of legislation directed toward the adjustment of social institutions to human needs. Trusts, factories, food, railroads, liquor selling and a hundred other subjects have been kept in the foreground of public attention. The American people might almost plead guilty to adjustment madness.

From the foundation of the earliest colonies, the basis, in theory at least, was laid for the development of the individual. The colonists believed in the worth-whileness of men, they lived in an age of natural philosophy; they were the products of an effort to secure religious and political freedom; they therefore emphasized the individual conscience, and the right of the individual to think and act for himself. Each individual was a man, to be so regarded, and so honored. Their new life was a hard one. Nature presented an aspect on the rocky, untilled New England coast different from that in the civilized countries of the old world. There was but one way to meet these new conditions—the individual must carve out his own future.

Throughout the United States, the watchword of the people has been opportunity. Without opportunity, the people perish—hence opportunity must stand waiting for each succeeding generation. In the turmoil of commercial life, in the ebb and flow of the immigrant tide, the reality has been frequently lost; yet the ideal of opportunity remains as firmly rooted as ever.

The worth-whileness of men, the social control of the environment, and a free opportunity for the development of the individual constitute the basis for social advance in the United States. The ideal is firmly rooted; the possibility of its realization is an everpresent reality.

With a boundless wealth of natural resources; bulwarked by the stock of the dominant races; with abundant leisure; granting freedom and individuality to women; foregoing war; cognizant of the principles of race making; Social Adjustment and of Education, the American nation is thrown into the foreground, as the land for the development of the Super Race. The American people have within their grasp the torch of social progress. Can they carry it in the van, lighting the dark caverns of the future? Can they develop a race of men who shall set a standard for the world—men of physical and mental power, efficient, broadly sympathetic, actuated by the highest ideals, striving toward a vision of human nobleness?

The answer rests with this and the succeeding generations. Given ten talents of opportunity, are we as a nation worthy to be made the rulers over ten cities? Provided with the raw stuff of a Super Race, can we mold it into "A mightier race than any that has been?" The past worked with things: the present works with men. "We stand at the verge of a state of culture, which will be that of the depths, not, as heretofore, of the surface alone; a stage which will not be merely a culture through mankind, but a culture of mankind. For the first time the great fashioners of culture will be able to work in marble instead of, as heretofore, being forced to work in snow."[23] Bulwarked by this pregnant thought, and assured by Ruskin that, "There is as yet no ascertained limit to the noblesse of person and mind which the human creature may attain," we press forward confidently, advocating and practicing those measures which will create the energy, mental grasp, efficiency, sympathy and vision of the Super Man and the Super Race.

Footnotes:

[1] JOHN RUSKIN, *Unto this Last*—Essay II.

[2] WILLIAM B. YEATS, *Poetic Works*, Vol. II, p. 407. Macmillan Co., N. Y.

[3] FREDERICK NIETZSCHE, *Thus Spoke Zarathustra*, pp. 5-296. Macmillan Co., N. Y.

[4] CARL SNYDER, *The World Machine*. New York, Longmans, Green & Co., 1907.

[5] PRESTONIA MANN MARTIN, *Is Mankind Advancing?* New York, Baker & Taylor Co., 1911.

[6] G. BERNARD SHAW, *Man and Super Man*, p. 218-219. N. Y., Brentano's.

[7] HERBERT SPENCER, *The Data of Ethics*. Para. 97. N. Y., D. Appleton & Co., 1893.

[8] SAML. Z. BATTEN, *The Redemption of the Unfit*, American Journal of Sociology, Vol. 14, p. 242 (1909).

[9] FRANCIS GALTON, *Memoirs of My Life*, p. 311. N. Y., E. P. Dutton, 1909.

[10] ARNOLD WHITE, *Efficiency and Empire*, p. 97. London, Methuen & Co., 1901.

[11] W. C. & C. D. WHETHAM, *The Family and the Nations*, p. 85. N. Y., Longmans, 1909.

[12] GUSTAVE MICHAUD, *Shall We Improve Our Race*, The Popular Science Monthly, Vol. 72, p. 77 (1908).

[13] J. A. THOMPSON, *Heredity*, p. 331. N. Y., G. P. Putnam's Sons, 1908.

[14] GUSTAVE MICHAUD, *Shall We Improve Our Race?* Popular Science Monthly, Vol. 72, p. 77 (1908).

[15] J. ARTHUR THOMPSON, *Heredity*, p. 308. N. Y., G. P. Putnam's Sons, 1908.

[16] LESTER F. WARD, *Applied Sociology*, pp. 224-282. Boston, Ginn & Co., 1906.

[17] For a more complete statement of the problem, see *Social Adjustment*, SCOTT NEARING, New York: Macmillan Company, 1911.

[18] ROBERT LOUIS STEVENSON, *Virginibus Puerisque*.

[19] WM. Z. RIPLEY, *Races of Europe*. N. Y., D. Appleton & Co., 1899.

[20] C. E. WOODRUFF, *The Expansion of Races*. N. Y., Rebman, 1909.

[21] D. S. JORDAN, *The Human Harvest*, p. 54. Boston, American Unitarian Association, 1907.

[22] *Ibid*, p. 48.

[23] ELLEN KEY, *Love and Marriage*, p. 53. N. Y., Putnam, 1911.

www.ingramcontent.com/pod-product-compliance
Ingram Content Group UK Ltd.
Pitfield, Milton Keynes, MK11 3LW, UK
UKHW041053100125
453365UK00005B/430